40 Pot Pie Recipes for Home

By: Kelly Johnson

Table of Contents

- Classic Chicken Pot Pie
- Beef and Mushroom Pot Pie
- Vegetarian Spinach and Feta Pot Pie
- Turkey and Cranberry Pot Pie
- Ham and Cheese Pot Pie
- Shrimp and Broccoli Pot Pie
- Lobster Pot Pie
- BBQ Pulled Pork Pot Pie
- Sweet Potato and Black Bean Pot Pie
- Buffalo Chicken Pot Pie
- Salmon and Dill Pot Pie
- Caprese Pot Pie with Tomatoes and Mozzarella
- Sausage and Peppers Pot Pie
- Vegetable Curry Pot Pie
- Chicken Alfredo Pot Pie
- Chili Cheese Pot Pie
- Ratatouille Pot Pie
- Teriyaki Chicken Pot Pie
- Buffalo Cauliflower Pot Pie
- Greek Spanakopita Pot Pie
- Chicken and Dumplings Pot Pie
- Margherita Pizza Pot Pie
- Tex-Mex Taco Pot Pie
- Philly Cheesesteak Pot Pie
- Mediterranean Chickpea Pot Pie
- Pesto Chicken Pot Pie
- Hawaiian Pizza Pot Pie
- Chicken Pesto Pot Pie
- Sloppy Joe Pot Pie
- Mushroom and Leek Pot Pie
- Spinach and Artichoke Pot Pie
- Italian Sausage and Peppers Pot Pie
- Bacon and Egg Breakfast Pot Pie
- Chicken and Waffle Pot Pie
- Buffalo Cauliflower Mac and Cheese Pot Pie

- Teriyaki Salmon Pot Pie
- Southwest Chicken Pot Pie
- Quiche Lorraine Pot Pie
- Cheesy Broccoli and Rice Pot Pie
- Caramelized Onion and Gruyere Pot Pie

Classic Chicken Pot Pie

Ingredients:

For the Filling:

- 2 cups cooked chicken, shredded or diced
- 1 cup frozen peas
- 1 cup carrots, diced
- 1/2 cup celery, diced
- 1/3 cup unsalted butter
- 1/3 cup all-purpose flour
- 1/2 teaspoon salt
- 1/4 teaspoon black pepper
- 1/4 teaspoon celery seed (optional)
- 1/4 teaspoon onion powder
- 1/4 teaspoon garlic powder
- 2 cups chicken broth
- 1 1/3 cups milk

For the Pie Crust:

- 1 package (2 crusts) store-bought or homemade pie crust

Instructions:

Preheat your oven to 425°F (220°C).
In a large saucepan, melt the butter over medium heat. Add the diced carrots, celery, and peas. Cook for about 5 minutes or until the vegetables are slightly tender.
Stir in the flour, salt, pepper, celery seed, onion powder, and garlic powder until well combined with the vegetables.
Gradually whisk in the chicken broth and milk, stirring constantly to avoid lumps. Cook the mixture until it thickens and becomes smooth, usually around 5-7 minutes.
Add the cooked chicken to the mixture and stir until everything is well combined. Remove the saucepan from heat.
Roll out one pie crust and place it into the bottom of a 9-inch pie dish. Pour the chicken mixture over the crust.

Roll out the second pie crust and place it over the filling. Seal the edges by crimping them with a fork or your fingers. Cut a few slits in the top crust to allow steam to escape.

Optional: Brush the top crust with a beaten egg for a golden finish.

Place the pie dish on a baking sheet to catch any potential drips and bake in the preheated oven for 30-35 minutes or until the crust is golden brown.

Allow the chicken pot pie to cool for a few minutes before serving. Enjoy your classic chicken pot pie!

Feel free to customize the recipe to your liking, and bon appétit!

Beef and Mushroom Pot Pie

Ingredients:

For the Filling:

- 1 1/2 pounds (680g) beef stew meat, cubed
- Salt and black pepper to taste
- 2 tablespoons olive oil
- 1 large onion, chopped
- 2 cloves garlic, minced
- 8 ounces (225g) mushrooms, sliced
- 1/4 cup all-purpose flour
- 2 cups beef broth
- 1 tablespoon tomato paste
- 1 teaspoon Worcestershire sauce
- 1 teaspoon dried thyme
- 1 cup frozen peas

For the Pie Crust:

- 1 package (2 crusts) store-bought or homemade pie crust

Instructions:

Preheat your oven to 425°F (220°C).

Season the beef stew meat with salt and black pepper. In a large skillet or Dutch oven, heat the olive oil over medium-high heat. Brown the beef cubes on all sides. Remove the beef from the skillet and set aside.

In the same skillet, add the chopped onion and cook until softened, about 3-5 minutes. Add the minced garlic and sliced mushrooms, cooking for an additional 3-4 minutes until the mushrooms release their moisture.

Sprinkle the flour over the vegetables and stir to combine. Cook for 1-2 minutes to eliminate the raw flour taste.

Gradually add the beef broth, stirring constantly to avoid lumps. Stir in the tomato paste, Worcestershire sauce, and dried thyme. Bring the mixture to a simmer, and then add the browned beef back to the skillet. Allow it to simmer for 10-15 minutes or until the beef is tender and the mixture thickens.

Stir in the frozen peas and cook for an additional 2 minutes. Adjust seasoning with salt and black pepper to taste. Remove the skillet from heat.

Roll out one pie crust and place it into the bottom of a 9-inch pie dish. Pour the beef and mushroom filling over the crust.

Roll out the second pie crust and place it over the filling. Seal the edges by crimping them with a fork or your fingers. Cut a few slits in the top crust to allow steam to escape.
Optional: Brush the top crust with a beaten egg for a golden finish.
Place the pie dish on a baking sheet to catch any potential drips and bake in the preheated oven for 30-35 minutes or until the crust is golden brown.
Allow the beef and mushroom pot pie to cool for a few minutes before serving. Enjoy your hearty and flavorful pot pie!

Feel free to adjust the recipe to suit your preferences, and happy cooking!

Vegetarian Spinach and Feta Pot Pie

Ingredients:

For the Filling:

- 2 tablespoons olive oil
- 1 medium onion, finely chopped
- 3 cloves garlic, minced
- 8 cups fresh spinach, chopped
- 1 cup feta cheese, crumbled
- 1/2 cup ricotta cheese
- 1/4 cup grated Parmesan cheese
- Salt and black pepper to taste
- 1 teaspoon dried oregano
- 1/2 teaspoon nutmeg (optional)
- Zest of one lemon
- 1 tablespoon lemon juice

For the Pie Crust:

- 1 package (2 crusts) store-bought or homemade pie crust

Instructions:

Preheat your oven to 425°F (220°C).

In a large skillet, heat olive oil over medium heat. Add chopped onion and cook until softened, about 3-5 minutes. Add minced garlic and cook for an additional 1-2 minutes.

Add the chopped spinach to the skillet in batches, allowing it to wilt. Cook until all the spinach is wilted and any excess moisture has evaporated.

In a large bowl, combine the cooked spinach and onions with crumbled feta, ricotta, Parmesan cheese, salt, black pepper, dried oregano, nutmeg (if using), lemon zest, and lemon juice. Mix well to combine.

Roll out one pie crust and place it into the bottom of a 9-inch pie dish. Spoon the spinach and feta mixture over the crust.

Roll out the second pie crust and place it over the filling. Seal the edges by crimping them with a fork or your fingers. Cut a few slits in the top crust to allow steam to escape.
Optional: Brush the top crust with a beaten egg for a golden finish.
Place the pie dish on a baking sheet to catch any potential drips and bake in the preheated oven for 30-35 minutes or until the crust is golden brown.
Allow the vegetarian spinach and feta pot pie to cool for a few minutes before serving. Enjoy this delicious and satisfying meatless option!

Feel free to customize the recipe according to your taste, and happy cooking!

Turkey and Cranberry Pot Pie

Ingredients:

For the Filling:

- 2 cups cooked turkey, shredded or diced
- 1 cup frozen cranberries
- 1 cup carrots, diced
- 1/2 cup celery, diced
- 1/3 cup unsalted butter
- 1/3 cup all-purpose flour
- 1/2 teaspoon salt
- 1/4 teaspoon black pepper
- 1/4 teaspoon dried thyme
- 2 cups turkey or chicken broth
- 1 1/3 cups milk

For the Pie Crust:

- 1 package (2 crusts) store-bought or homemade pie crust

Instructions:

Preheat your oven to 425°F (220°C).
In a large saucepan, melt the butter over medium heat. Add the diced carrots and celery. Cook for about 5 minutes or until the vegetables are slightly tender.
Stir in the flour, salt, black pepper, and dried thyme until well combined with the vegetables.
Gradually whisk in the turkey or chicken broth and milk, stirring constantly to avoid lumps. Cook the mixture until it thickens and becomes smooth, usually around 5-7 minutes.
Add the cooked turkey and frozen cranberries to the mixture and stir until everything is well combined. Remove the saucepan from heat.
Roll out one pie crust and place it into the bottom of a 9-inch pie dish. Pour the turkey and cranberry filling over the crust.
Roll out the second pie crust and place it over the filling. Seal the edges by crimping them with a fork or your fingers. Cut a few slits in the top crust to allow steam to escape.

Optional: Brush the top crust with a beaten egg for a golden finish.
Place the pie dish on a baking sheet to catch any potential drips and bake in the preheated oven for 30-35 minutes or until the crust is golden brown.
Allow the turkey and cranberry pot pie to cool for a few minutes before serving.
Enjoy the festive flavors of this delicious pot pie!

Feel free to modify the recipe to your liking, and happy cooking!

Ham and Cheese Pot Pie

Ingredients:

For the Filling:

- 2 cups cooked ham, diced
- 1 cup sharp cheddar cheese, shredded
- 1/2 cup Swiss cheese, shredded
- 1/2 cup frozen peas
- 1/4 cup unsalted butter
- 1/4 cup all-purpose flour
- 1/2 teaspoon Dijon mustard
- 1/4 teaspoon black pepper
- 1 1/2 cups milk
- 1/2 cup chicken or vegetable broth

For the Pie Crust:

- 1 package (2 crusts) store-bought or homemade pie crust

Instructions:

Preheat your oven to 425°F (220°C).
In a large saucepan, melt the butter over medium heat. Add the diced ham and cook for about 3-4 minutes until lightly browned.
Stir in the flour, Dijon mustard, and black pepper until well combined with the ham.
Gradually whisk in the milk and chicken or vegetable broth, stirring constantly to avoid lumps. Cook the mixture until it thickens and becomes smooth, usually around 5-7 minutes.
Add the shredded cheddar and Swiss cheese to the mixture, stirring until melted and well combined. Stir in the frozen peas. Remove the saucepan from heat.
Roll out one pie crust and place it into the bottom of a 9-inch pie dish. Pour the ham and cheese filling over the crust.
Roll out the second pie crust and place it over the filling. Seal the edges by crimping them with a fork or your fingers. Cut a few slits in the top crust to allow steam to escape.
Optional: Brush the top crust with a beaten egg for a golden finish.

Place the pie dish on a baking sheet to catch any potential drips and bake in the preheated oven for 30-35 minutes or until the crust is golden brown.

Allow the ham and cheese pot pie to cool for a few minutes before serving. Enjoy the savory goodness of this delicious pot pie!

Feel free to adjust the recipe to your preferences, and happy cooking!

Shrimp and Broccoli Pot Pie

Ingredients:

For the Filling:

- 1 pound large shrimp, peeled and deveined
- 2 cups broccoli florets, blanched
- 1/2 cup red bell pepper, diced
- 1/4 cup unsalted butter
- 1/4 cup all-purpose flour
- 1/2 teaspoon garlic powder
- 1/2 teaspoon onion powder
- 1/2 teaspoon dried thyme
- 1/4 teaspoon black pepper
- 1 1/2 cups chicken or vegetable broth
- 1 cup whole milk
- 1/4 cup grated Parmesan cheese
- Salt to taste

For the Pie Crust:

- 1 package (2 crusts) store-bought or homemade pie crust

Instructions:

Preheat your oven to 425°F (220°C).

In a large skillet, melt the butter over medium heat. Add the diced red bell pepper and cook for about 2-3 minutes until softened.

Add the shrimp to the skillet and cook for 2-3 minutes or until they turn pink and opaque. Remove the shrimp and bell pepper from the skillet and set aside.

In the same skillet, add the flour, garlic powder, onion powder, dried thyme, and black pepper. Stir continuously to form a roux. Cook for 1-2 minutes to eliminate the raw flour taste.

Gradually whisk in the chicken or vegetable broth and milk, stirring constantly to avoid lumps. Continue cooking until the mixture thickens.

Stir in the grated Parmesan cheese until melted and smooth. Season with salt to taste.

Add the cooked shrimp, blanched broccoli, and red bell pepper back to the skillet. Mix until the shrimp and vegetables are well-coated with the sauce. Remove the skillet from heat.

Roll out one pie crust and place it into the bottom of a 9-inch pie dish. Pour the shrimp and broccoli filling over the crust.

Roll out the second pie crust and place it over the filling. Seal the edges by crimping them with a fork or your fingers. Cut a few slits in the top crust to allow steam to escape.

Optional: Brush the top crust with a beaten egg for a golden finish.

Place the pie dish on a baking sheet to catch any potential drips and bake in the preheated oven for 30-35 minutes or until the crust is golden brown.

Allow the shrimp and broccoli pot pie to cool for a few minutes before serving.

Enjoy the delightful combination of flavors in this seafood-inspired pot pie!

Feel free to adjust the recipe according to your taste preferences, and happy cooking!

Lobster Pot Pie

Ingredients:

For the Filling:

- 1 1/2 pounds lobster meat, cooked and chopped into bite-sized pieces
- 1 cup frozen peas
- 1/2 cup corn kernels (fresh or frozen)
- 1/4 cup unsalted butter
- 1/4 cup all-purpose flour
- 1/2 cup onion, finely chopped
- 1/2 cup celery, finely chopped
- 1/2 cup carrots, finely chopped
- 2 cloves garlic, minced
- 1/4 cup dry white wine (optional)
- 1 1/2 cups seafood or vegetable broth
- 1 cup heavy cream
- 1/4 cup fresh parsley, chopped
- Salt and black pepper to taste

For the Pie Crust:

- 1 package (2 crusts) store-bought or homemade pie crust

Instructions:

Preheat your oven to 425°F (220°C).
In a large skillet or Dutch oven, melt the butter over medium heat. Add the chopped onion, celery, carrots, and minced garlic. Cook for about 5-7 minutes or until the vegetables are softened.
Sprinkle the flour over the vegetables and stir to create a roux. Cook for an additional 2-3 minutes to eliminate the raw flour taste.
If using white wine, pour it into the skillet and stir, scraping the bottom of the pan to incorporate any flavorful bits. Cook for 2-3 minutes until the wine reduces.
Gradually whisk in the seafood or vegetable broth and heavy cream, stirring constantly to avoid lumps. Cook the mixture until it thickens and becomes smooth, usually around 5-7 minutes.

Add the cooked and chopped lobster meat, frozen peas, corn, chopped parsley, salt, and black pepper to the mixture. Stir until all the ingredients are well combined. Adjust seasoning to taste.

Roll out one pie crust and place it into the bottom of a 9-inch pie dish. Pour the lobster filling over the crust.

Roll out the second pie crust and place it over the filling. Seal the edges by crimping them with a fork or your fingers. Cut a few slits in the top crust to allow steam to escape.

Optional: Brush the top crust with a beaten egg for a golden finish.

Place the pie dish on a baking sheet to catch any potential drips and bake in the preheated oven for 30-35 minutes or until the crust is golden brown.

Allow the lobster pot pie to cool for a few minutes before serving. Enjoy the luxurious and savory flavors of this special pot pie!

Feel free to customize the recipe based on your preferences, and happy indulging!

BBQ Pulled Pork Pot Pie

Ingredients:

For the Filling:

- 3 cups cooked and shredded BBQ pulled pork
- 1 cup corn kernels (fresh or frozen)
- 1/2 cup red bell pepper, diced
- 1/2 cup onion, finely chopped
- 1/2 cup barbecue sauce
- 1/4 cup unsalted butter
- 1/4 cup all-purpose flour
- 1 1/2 cups chicken or vegetable broth
- 1/2 cup milk
- 1 teaspoon smoked paprika
- Salt and black pepper to taste

For the Pie Crust:

- 1 package (2 crusts) store-bought or homemade pie crust

Instructions:

Preheat your oven to 425°F (220°C).
In a large skillet, melt the butter over medium heat. Add the chopped onion and red bell pepper. Cook for about 3-5 minutes until softened.
Stir in the flour and smoked paprika, creating a roux. Cook for an additional 2-3 minutes to eliminate the raw flour taste.
Gradually whisk in the chicken or vegetable broth and milk, stirring constantly to avoid lumps. Cook the mixture until it thickens and becomes smooth, usually around 5-7 minutes.
Add the shredded BBQ pulled pork, corn kernels, barbecue sauce, salt, and black pepper to the mixture. Stir until all ingredients are well combined. Adjust seasoning to taste.
Roll out one pie crust and place it into the bottom of a 9-inch pie dish. Pour the BBQ pulled pork filling over the crust.

Roll out the second pie crust and place it over the filling. Seal the edges by crimping them with a fork or your fingers. Cut a few slits in the top crust to allow steam to escape.

Optional: Brush the top crust with a beaten egg for a golden finish.

Place the pie dish on a baking sheet to catch any potential drips and bake in the preheated oven for 30-35 minutes or until the crust is golden brown.

Allow the BBQ pulled pork pot pie to cool for a few minutes before serving. Enjoy the smoky and savory flavors of this delicious pot pie!

Feel free to personalize the recipe to your liking, and happy cooking!

Sweet Potato and Black Bean Pot Pie

Ingredients:

For the Filling:

- 2 medium sweet potatoes, peeled and diced
- 1 can (15 ounces) black beans, drained and rinsed
- 1 cup corn kernels (fresh or frozen)
- 1/2 cup red bell pepper, diced
- 1/2 cup onion, finely chopped
- 2 cloves garlic, minced
- 2 tablespoons olive oil
- 1 teaspoon ground cumin
- 1 teaspoon chili powder
- 1/2 teaspoon smoked paprika
- Salt and black pepper to taste
- 1/2 cup vegetable broth
- 1 tablespoon lime juice
- 1/4 cup fresh cilantro, chopped

For the Pie Crust:

- 1 package (2 crusts) store-bought or homemade pie crust

Instructions:

Preheat your oven to 425°F (220°C).
In a large skillet, heat olive oil over medium heat. Add the chopped onion and red bell pepper. Cook for about 3-5 minutes until softened.
Add the diced sweet potatoes to the skillet and cook for an additional 5-7 minutes until they begin to soften.
Stir in the minced garlic, ground cumin, chili powder, smoked paprika, salt, and black pepper. Cook for 1-2 minutes until the spices are fragrant.
Add the black beans, corn, vegetable broth, and lime juice to the skillet. Stir and cook until the sweet potatoes are tender, and the mixture is well combined.
Remove from heat and stir in the chopped cilantro.
Roll out one pie crust and place it into the bottom of a 9-inch pie dish. Spoon the sweet potato and black bean filling over the crust.

Roll out the second pie crust and place it over the filling. Seal the edges by crimping them with a fork or your fingers. Cut a few slits in the top crust to allow steam to escape.

Optional: Brush the top crust with a beaten egg for a golden finish.

Place the pie dish on a baking sheet to catch any potential drips and bake in the preheated oven for 30-35 minutes or until the crust is golden brown.

Allow the sweet potato and black bean pot pie to cool for a few minutes before serving. Enjoy this flavorful and hearty vegetarian pot pie!

Feel free to adjust the recipe to suit your preferences, and happy cooking!

Buffalo Chicken Pot Pie

Ingredients:

For the Filling:

- 2 cups cooked and shredded chicken (rotisserie or cooked chicken breasts)
- 1/2 cup celery, finely chopped
- 1/2 cup carrots, finely chopped
- 1/2 cup onion, finely chopped
- 1/3 cup unsalted butter
- 1/3 cup all-purpose flour
- 1 teaspoon garlic powder
- 1 teaspoon onion powder
- 1/2 teaspoon celery seed
- 1/2 cup buffalo wing sauce
- 1 cup chicken broth
- 1/2 cup whole milk
- Salt and black pepper to taste

For the Pie Crust:

- 1 package (2 crusts) store-bought or homemade pie crust

Instructions:

Preheat your oven to 425°F (220°C).
In a large skillet, melt the butter over medium heat. Add the chopped celery, carrots, and onion. Cook for about 5-7 minutes until the vegetables are softened. Stir in the flour, garlic powder, onion powder, and celery seed. Cook for an additional 2-3 minutes to create a roux.
Gradually whisk in the buffalo wing sauce, chicken broth, and whole milk, stirring constantly to avoid lumps. Cook the mixture until it thickens and becomes smooth, usually around 5-7 minutes.
Add the shredded chicken to the skillet and stir until the chicken is well coated with the buffalo sauce mixture. Season with salt and black pepper to taste. Remove the skillet from heat.

Roll out one pie crust and place it into the bottom of a 9-inch pie dish. Pour the buffalo chicken filling over the crust.

Roll out the second pie crust and place it over the filling. Seal the edges by crimping them with a fork or your fingers. Cut a few slits in the top crust to allow steam to escape.

Optional: Brush the top crust with a beaten egg for a golden finish.

Place the pie dish on a baking sheet to catch any potential drips and bake in the preheated oven for 30-35 minutes or until the crust is golden brown.

Allow the buffalo chicken pot pie to cool for a few minutes before serving. Enjoy the spicy and tangy flavors of this delicious pot pie!

Feel free to customize the recipe to your liking, and happy cooking!

Salmon and Dill Pot Pie

Ingredients:

For the Filling:

- 1 pound salmon fillets, skinless and boneless, cut into bite-sized pieces
- 1 cup potatoes, diced
- 1/2 cup carrots, diced
- 1/2 cup celery, diced
- 1/4 cup unsalted butter
- 1/4 cup all-purpose flour
- 1 cup chicken or vegetable broth
- 1 cup whole milk
- 2 tablespoons fresh dill, chopped
- 1 tablespoon lemon juice
- Salt and black pepper to taste

For the Pie Crust:

- 1 package (2 crusts) store-bought or homemade pie crust

Instructions:

Preheat your oven to 425°F (220°C).
In a medium saucepan, bring water to a boil. Add the diced potatoes and carrots and cook for about 5 minutes or until they start to become tender. Drain and set aside.
In a large skillet, melt the butter over medium heat. Add the diced celery and cook for about 3-5 minutes until softened.
Stir in the flour, creating a roux. Cook for an additional 2-3 minutes to eliminate the raw flour taste.
Gradually whisk in the chicken or vegetable broth and whole milk, stirring constantly to avoid lumps. Cook the mixture until it thickens and becomes smooth, usually around 5-7 minutes.
Add the diced salmon, blanched potatoes, carrots, chopped dill, lemon juice, salt, and black pepper to the skillet. Stir gently to combine all ingredients. Remove from heat.

Roll out one pie crust and place it into the bottom of a 9-inch pie dish. Pour the salmon and dill filling over the crust.

Roll out the second pie crust and place it over the filling. Seal the edges by crimping them with a fork or your fingers. Cut a few slits in the top crust to allow steam to escape.

Optional: Brush the top crust with a beaten egg for a golden finish.

Place the pie dish on a baking sheet to catch any potential drips and bake in the preheated oven for 30-35 minutes or until the crust is golden brown.

Allow the salmon and dill pot pie to cool for a few minutes before serving. Enjoy the delicate flavors of this delightful seafood pot pie!

Feel free to adjust the recipe to suit your preferences, and happy cooking!

Caprese Pot Pie with Tomatoes and Mozzarella

Ingredients:

For the Filling:

- 3 cups cherry tomatoes, halved
- 2 cups fresh mozzarella, diced
- 1/4 cup fresh basil leaves, chopped
- 2 tablespoons balsamic glaze
- 3 tablespoons extra virgin olive oil
- Salt and black pepper to taste

For the Pie Crust:

- 1 package (2 crusts) store-bought or homemade pie crust

Instructions:

Preheat your oven to 425°F (220°C).
In a large bowl, combine the cherry tomatoes, fresh mozzarella, chopped basil, balsamic glaze, extra virgin olive oil, salt, and black pepper. Toss gently until all ingredients are well coated.
Roll out one pie crust and place it into the bottom of a 9-inch pie dish.
Spoon the caprese filling mixture over the crust, spreading it evenly.
Roll out the second pie crust and place it over the filling. Seal the edges by crimping them with a fork or your fingers. Cut a few slits in the top crust to allow steam to escape.
Optional: Brush the top crust with a little extra virgin olive oil for a golden finish.
Place the pie dish on a baking sheet to catch any potential drips and bake in the preheated oven for 25-30 minutes or until the crust is golden brown.
Allow the Caprese pot pie to cool for a few minutes before serving. This pot pie is best served warm to preserve the fresh flavors of the tomatoes, mozzarella, and basil.

Enjoy this unique and flavorful twist on the classic pot pie with the delicious combination of Caprese ingredients! Feel free to customize the recipe to your liking, and happy cooking!

Sausage and Peppers Pot Pie

Ingredients:

For the Filling:

- 1 pound Italian sausage, casings removed
- 1 cup bell peppers (mix of red, green, and yellow), sliced
- 1 cup onion, sliced
- 2 cloves garlic, minced
- 1 can (14 ounces) diced tomatoes, drained
- 1 cup shredded mozzarella cheese
- 1/4 cup grated Parmesan cheese
- 1 teaspoon dried oregano
- 1 teaspoon dried basil
- Salt and black pepper to taste

For the Pie Crust:

- 1 package (2 crusts) store-bought or homemade pie crust

Instructions:

Preheat your oven to 425°F (220°C).
In a large skillet over medium heat, cook the Italian sausage, breaking it apart with a spoon as it cooks, until browned and cooked through. Drain any excess fat.
Add the sliced bell peppers, onion, and minced garlic to the skillet with the cooked sausage. Cook for about 5-7 minutes until the vegetables are softened.
Stir in the drained diced tomatoes, dried oregano, dried basil, salt, and black pepper. Cook for an additional 2-3 minutes, allowing the flavors to meld.
Remove the skillet from heat and let the mixture cool slightly. Stir in the shredded mozzarella and grated Parmesan cheese.
Roll out one pie crust and place it into the bottom of a 9-inch pie dish.
Spoon the sausage and peppers filling over the crust.

Roll out the second pie crust and place it over the filling. Seal the edges by crimping them with a fork or your fingers. Cut a few slits in the top crust to allow steam to escape.
Optional: Brush the top crust with a beaten egg for a golden finish.
Place the pie dish on a baking sheet to catch any potential drips and bake in the preheated oven for 30-35 minutes or until the crust is golden brown.
Allow the sausage and peppers pot pie to cool for a few minutes before serving.
Enjoy the hearty and flavorful combination of sausage, peppers, and cheese!

Feel free to customize the recipe to your preferences, and happy cooking!

Vegetable Curry Pot Pie

Ingredients:

For the Filling:

- 2 tablespoons vegetable oil
- 1 large onion, chopped
- 2 cloves garlic, minced
- 1 tablespoon ginger, minced
- 2 medium carrots, diced
- 1 cup potatoes, diced
- 1 cup cauliflower florets
- 1 cup green beans, cut into bite-sized pieces
- 1 cup peas (fresh or frozen)
- 1 can (14 ounces) chickpeas, drained and rinsed
- 1/4 cup all-purpose flour
- 2 tablespoons curry powder
- 1 teaspoon ground cumin
- 1 teaspoon ground coriander
- 1/2 teaspoon turmeric
- 1/4 teaspoon cayenne pepper (adjust to taste)
- 1 can (14 ounces) coconut milk
- 1 cup vegetable broth
- Salt and black pepper to taste
- Fresh cilantro, chopped (for garnish)

For the Pie Crust:

- 1 package (2 crusts) store-bought or homemade pie crust

Instructions:

Preheat your oven to 425°F (220°C).
In a large skillet, heat vegetable oil over medium heat. Add the chopped onion, minced garlic, and minced ginger. Cook for 2-3 minutes until the onions are softened.
Add the diced carrots, potatoes, cauliflower, green beans, peas, and chickpeas to the skillet. Cook for an additional 5-7 minutes until the vegetables start to soften.

Sprinkle the flour, curry powder, ground cumin, ground coriander, turmeric, and cayenne pepper over the vegetables. Stir to coat the vegetables evenly.

Gradually pour in the coconut milk and vegetable broth, stirring constantly to avoid lumps. Cook until the mixture thickens and the vegetables are fully cooked, about 8-10 minutes.

Season the filling with salt and black pepper to taste. Remove the skillet from heat and let the curry filling cool slightly.

Roll out one pie crust and place it into the bottom of a 9-inch pie dish.

Spoon the vegetable curry filling over the crust.

Roll out the second pie crust and place it over the filling. Seal the edges by crimping them with a fork or your fingers. Cut a few slits in the top crust to allow steam to escape.

Optional: Brush the top crust with a beaten egg for a golden finish.

Place the pie dish on a baking sheet to catch any potential drips and bake in the preheated oven for 30-35 minutes or until the crust is golden brown.

Allow the vegetable curry pot pie to cool for a few minutes before serving.

Garnish with chopped fresh cilantro before serving. Enjoy the rich and aromatic flavors of this vegetarian curry pot pie!

Feel free to customize the recipe to your liking, and happy cooking!

Chicken Alfredo Pot Pie

Ingredients:

For the Filling:

- 2 cups cooked chicken, shredded or diced
- 1 cup broccoli florets, blanched
- 1/2 cup mushrooms, sliced
- 1/4 cup unsalted butter
- 1/4 cup all-purpose flour
- 1 1/2 cups chicken broth
- 1 1/2 cups heavy cream
- 1 cup grated Parmesan cheese
- 1 teaspoon garlic powder
- Salt and black pepper to taste
- 1 tablespoon fresh parsley, chopped (for garnish)

For the Pie Crust:

- 1 package (2 crusts) store-bought or homemade pie crust

Instructions:

Preheat your oven to 425°F (220°C).

In a large skillet, melt the butter over medium heat. Add the sliced mushrooms and cook until they release their moisture and become golden brown, about 5-7 minutes.

Sprinkle the flour over the mushrooms and stir to create a roux. Cook for an additional 2-3 minutes to eliminate the raw flour taste.

Gradually whisk in the chicken broth and heavy cream, stirring constantly to avoid lumps. Cook the mixture until it thickens and becomes smooth, usually around 5-7 minutes.

Stir in the grated Parmesan cheese, garlic powder, salt, and black pepper. Continue stirring until the cheese is melted and the sauce is well combined.

Add the cooked chicken and blanched broccoli to the skillet, stirring until the ingredients are coated with the Alfredo sauce. Remove the skillet from heat.

Roll out one pie crust and place it into the bottom of a 9-inch pie dish.

Pour the chicken Alfredo filling over the crust.

Roll out the second pie crust and place it over the filling. Seal the edges by crimping them with a fork or your fingers. Cut a few slits in the top crust to allow steam to escape.
Optional: Brush the top crust with a beaten egg for a golden finish.
Place the pie dish on a baking sheet to catch any potential drips and bake in the preheated oven for 30-35 minutes or until the crust is golden brown.
Allow the chicken Alfredo pot pie to cool for a few minutes before serving.
Garnish with chopped fresh parsley before serving. Enjoy the creamy and comforting flavors of this Alfredo-inspired pot pie!

Feel free to customize the recipe to your liking, and happy cooking!

Chili Cheese Pot Pie

Ingredients:

For the Filling:

- 1 pound ground beef or turkey
- 1 onion, finely chopped
- 2 cloves garlic, minced
- 1 can (15 ounces) kidney beans, drained and rinsed
- 1 can (14 ounces) diced tomatoes, undrained
- 1 can (6 ounces) tomato paste
- 1 cup corn kernels (fresh or frozen)
- 1 tablespoon chili powder
- 1 teaspoon ground cumin
- 1/2 teaspoon smoked paprika
- Salt and black pepper to taste
- 1 cup shredded cheddar cheese

For the Pie Crust:

- 1 package (2 crusts) store-bought or homemade pie crust

Instructions:

Preheat your oven to 425°F (220°C).

In a large skillet, cook the ground beef or turkey over medium heat until browned. Drain any excess fat.

Add the chopped onion and minced garlic to the skillet. Cook for about 3-5 minutes until the onion is softened.

Stir in the kidney beans, diced tomatoes, tomato paste, corn kernels, chili powder, ground cumin, smoked paprika, salt, and black pepper. Cook for an additional 5-7 minutes, allowing the flavors to meld.

Remove the skillet from heat and let the chili mixture cool slightly. Stir in the shredded cheddar cheese.

Roll out one pie crust and place it into the bottom of a 9-inch pie dish.

Spoon the chili cheese filling over the crust.

Roll out the second pie crust and place it over the filling. Seal the edges by crimping them with a fork or your fingers. Cut a few slits in the top crust to allow steam to escape.

Optional: Brush the top crust with a beaten egg for a golden finish.

Place the pie dish on a baking sheet to catch any potential drips and bake in the preheated oven for 30-35 minutes or until the crust is golden brown.

Allow the chili cheese pot pie to cool for a few minutes before serving. Enjoy the hearty and cheesy goodness of this comfort food!

Feel free to customize the recipe by adding your favorite chili toppings or adjusting the spice level to suit your taste. Happy cooking!

Ratatouille Pot Pie

Ingredients:

For the Filling:

- 1 eggplant, diced
- 2 zucchini, diced
- 1 yellow bell pepper, diced
- 1 red bell pepper, diced
- 1 onion, finely chopped
- 2 cloves garlic, minced
- 1 can (14 ounces) diced tomatoes, drained
- 2 tablespoons tomato paste
- 1 teaspoon dried thyme
- 1 teaspoon dried rosemary
- Salt and black pepper to taste
- 1/4 cup fresh basil, chopped
- 1/4 cup fresh parsley, chopped
- 2 tablespoons olive oil

For the Pie Crust:

- 1 package (2 crusts) store-bought or homemade pie crust

Instructions:

Preheat your oven to 425°F (220°C).

In a large skillet, heat the olive oil over medium heat. Add the chopped onion and minced garlic. Cook for 3-5 minutes until the onion is softened.

Add the diced eggplant, zucchini, yellow bell pepper, and red bell pepper to the skillet. Cook for about 10-12 minutes, stirring occasionally, until the vegetables are tender.

Stir in the drained diced tomatoes, tomato paste, dried thyme, dried rosemary, salt, and black pepper. Cook for an additional 5 minutes, allowing the flavors to blend. Remove the skillet from heat.

Stir in the fresh basil and parsley. Adjust seasoning to taste.

Roll out one pie crust and place it into the bottom of a 9-inch pie dish.
Spoon the ratatouille filling over the crust.
Roll out the second pie crust and place it over the filling. Seal the edges by crimping them with a fork or your fingers. Cut a few slits in the top crust to allow steam to escape.
Optional: Brush the top crust with a beaten egg for a golden finish.
Place the pie dish on a baking sheet to catch any potential drips and bake in the preheated oven for 30-35 minutes or until the crust is golden brown.
Allow the ratatouille pot pie to cool for a few minutes before serving. Enjoy this delightful and colorful twist on the classic pot pie!

Feel free to customize the recipe to your liking, and happy cooking!

Teriyaki Chicken Pot Pie

Ingredients:

For the Filling:

- 1 eggplant, diced
- 2 zucchini, diced
- 1 yellow bell pepper, diced
- 1 red bell pepper, diced
- 1 onion, finely chopped
- 2 cloves garlic, minced
- 1 can (14 ounces) diced tomatoes, drained
- 2 tablespoons tomato paste
- 1 teaspoon dried thyme
- 1 teaspoon dried rosemary
- Salt and black pepper to taste
- 1/4 cup fresh basil, chopped
- 1/4 cup fresh parsley, chopped
- 2 tablespoons olive oil

For the Pie Crust:

- 1 package (2 crusts) store-bought or homemade pie crust

Instructions:

Preheat your oven to 425°F (220°C).
In a large skillet, heat the olive oil over medium heat. Add the chopped onion and minced garlic. Cook for 3-5 minutes until the onion is softened.
Add the diced eggplant, zucchini, yellow bell pepper, and red bell pepper to the skillet. Cook for about 10-12 minutes, stirring occasionally, until the vegetables are tender.
Stir in the drained diced tomatoes, tomato paste, dried thyme, dried rosemary, salt, and black pepper. Cook for an additional 5 minutes, allowing the flavors to blend. Remove the skillet from heat.
Stir in the fresh basil and parsley. Adjust seasoning to taste.

Roll out one pie crust and place it into the bottom of a 9-inch pie dish.
Spoon the ratatouille filling over the crust.
Roll out the second pie crust and place it over the filling. Seal the edges by crimping them with a fork or your fingers. Cut a few slits in the top crust to allow steam to escape.
Optional: Brush the top crust with a beaten egg for a golden finish.
Place the pie dish on a baking sheet to catch any potential drips and bake in the preheated oven for 30-35 minutes or until the crust is golden brown.
Allow the ratatouille pot pie to cool for a few minutes before serving. Enjoy this delightful and colorful twist on the classic pot pie!

Feel free to customize the recipe to your liking, and happy cooking!

Buffalo Cauliflower Pot Pie

Ingredients:

For the Filling:

- 1 head cauliflower, cut into bite-sized florets
- 1/2 cup buffalo sauce
- 3 tablespoons unsalted butter, melted
- 1 tablespoon white vinegar
- 1 teaspoon garlic powder
- 1 teaspoon onion powder
- 1/2 teaspoon smoked paprika
- Salt and black pepper to taste
- 1/4 cup blue cheese, crumbled (optional)

For the Pie Crust:

- 1 package (2 crusts) store-bought or homemade pie crust

Instructions:

Preheat your oven to 425°F (220°C).
In a large bowl, whisk together the melted butter, buffalo sauce, white vinegar, garlic powder, onion powder, smoked paprika, salt, and black pepper.
Add the cauliflower florets to the bowl, tossing them until well coated with the buffalo sauce mixture.
Spread the buffalo cauliflower on a baking sheet in a single layer. Roast in the preheated oven for 20-25 minutes or until the cauliflower is tender and slightly crispy.
Remove the cauliflower from the oven and let it cool slightly. If using blue cheese, gently fold it into the roasted cauliflower.
Roll out one pie crust and place it into the bottom of a 9-inch pie dish.
Spoon the buffalo cauliflower filling over the crust.
Roll out the second pie crust and place it over the filling. Seal the edges by crimping them with a fork or your fingers. Cut a few slits in the top crust to allow steam to escape.
Optional: Brush the top crust with a little extra buffalo sauce for added flavor.

Place the pie dish on a baking sheet to catch any potential drips and bake in the preheated oven for 30-35 minutes or until the crust is golden brown.
Allow the buffalo cauliflower pot pie to cool for a few minutes before serving.
Enjoy the spicy and tangy flavors of this unique and vegetarian-friendly pot pie!

Feel free to customize the recipe to your liking, and happy cooking!

Greek Spanakopita Pot Pie

Ingredients:

For the Filling:

- 1 pound fresh spinach, chopped
- 1 cup feta cheese, crumbled
- 1 cup ricotta cheese
- 1/2 cup grated Parmesan cheese
- 1/2 cup red onion, finely chopped
- 3 cloves garlic, minced
- 2 tablespoons olive oil
- 2 tablespoons fresh dill, chopped
- 1 teaspoon dried oregano
- Salt and black pepper to taste
- Zest of 1 lemon

For the Pie Crust:

- 1 package (2 crusts) store-bought or homemade pie crust

Instructions:

Preheat your oven to 425°F (220°C).
In a large skillet, heat olive oil over medium heat. Add the chopped red onion and minced garlic. Cook for 3-5 minutes until the onion is softened.
Add the chopped spinach to the skillet and cook until wilted, about 5-7 minutes. Drain any excess liquid from the spinach.
In a large bowl, combine the cooked spinach, crumbled feta cheese, ricotta cheese, Parmesan cheese, fresh dill, dried oregano, salt, black pepper, and lemon zest. Mix well to ensure all ingredients are evenly distributed.
Roll out one pie crust and place it into the bottom of a 9-inch pie dish.
Spoon the spanakopita filling over the crust.
Roll out the second pie crust and place it over the filling. Seal the edges by crimping them with a fork or your fingers. Cut a few slits in the top crust to allow steam to escape.

Optional: Brush the top crust with a beaten egg for a golden finish.
Place the pie dish on a baking sheet to catch any potential drips and bake in the preheated oven for 30-35 minutes or until the crust is golden brown.
Allow the Greek spanakopita pot pie to cool for a few minutes before serving.
Enjoy the rich and savory flavors of this Mediterranean-inspired pot pie!

Feel free to customize the recipe to your liking, and happy cooking!

Chicken and Dumplings Pot Pie

Ingredients:

For the Filling:

- 1 1/2 pounds boneless, skinless chicken breasts, cooked and shredded
- 1 cup carrots, diced
- 1 cup celery, diced
- 1/2 cup frozen peas
- 1/2 cup unsalted butter
- 1/2 cup all-purpose flour
- 4 cups chicken broth
- 1 cup whole milk
- 2 teaspoons dried thyme
- Salt and black pepper to taste

For the Dumplings:

- 2 cups all-purpose flour
- 1 tablespoon baking powder
- 1 teaspoon salt
- 1 cup buttermilk
- 1/2 cup unsalted butter, melted

Instructions:

Preheat your oven to 425°F (220°C).
In a large pot, melt the butter over medium heat. Add the diced carrots, celery, and frozen peas. Cook for about 5-7 minutes until the vegetables are softened. Stir in the flour to create a roux. Cook for an additional 2-3 minutes to eliminate the raw flour taste.
Gradually whisk in the chicken broth and whole milk, stirring constantly to avoid lumps. Cook the mixture until it thickens and becomes smooth, usually around 5-7 minutes.
Add the shredded chicken, dried thyme, salt, and black pepper to the pot. Stir until all ingredients are well combined. Remove the pot from heat.

In a separate bowl, whisk together the flour, baking powder, and salt for the dumplings.

Pour in the buttermilk and melted butter, stirring until just combined. Do not overmix.

Drop spoonfuls of the dumpling batter onto the surface of the chicken filling. Leave some space between the dumplings as they will expand during baking.

Place the pot in the preheated oven and bake for 20-25 minutes or until the dumplings are golden brown and cooked through.

Allow the chicken and dumplings pot pie to cool for a few minutes before serving. Enjoy the comforting and homey flavors of this classic dish!

Feel free to customize the recipe to your liking, and happy cooking!

Margherita Pizza Pot Pie

Ingredients:

For the Filling:

- 2 cups cherry tomatoes, halved
- 1 1/2 cups fresh mozzarella, diced
- 1/4 cup fresh basil leaves, torn
- 2 tablespoons extra virgin olive oil
- 2 cloves garlic, minced
- Salt and black pepper to taste
- 1/4 cup grated Parmesan cheese

For the Pie Crust:

- 1 package (2 crusts) store-bought or homemade pie crust

For Garnish:

- Extra fresh basil leaves
- Balsamic glaze (optional)

Instructions:

Preheat your oven to 425°F (220°C).
In a large bowl, combine the halved cherry tomatoes, diced fresh mozzarella, torn basil leaves, minced garlic, extra virgin olive oil, salt, and black pepper. Gently toss to coat the ingredients evenly.
Roll out one pie crust and place it into the bottom of a 9-inch pie dish.
Spoon the Margherita pizza filling over the crust.
Roll out the second pie crust and place it over the filling. Seal the edges by crimping them with a fork or your fingers. Cut a few slits in the top crust to allow steam to escape.
Sprinkle the grated Parmesan cheese over the top crust.
Optional: Brush the top crust with a little extra virgin olive oil for a golden finish.

Place the pie dish on a baking sheet to catch any potential drips and bake in the preheated oven for 25-30 minutes or until the crust is golden brown.
Allow the Margherita pizza pot pie to cool for a few minutes before serving.
Garnish with extra fresh basil leaves and drizzle with balsamic glaze if desired.
Slice and enjoy the delightful flavors of this pizza-inspired pot pie!

Feel free to customize the recipe by adding your favorite pizza toppings or adjusting the seasoning to your taste. Happy cooking!

Tex-Mex Taco Pot Pie

Ingredients:

For the Filling:

- 1 pound ground beef or turkey
- 1 onion, finely chopped
- 2 cloves garlic, minced
- 1 packet taco seasoning
- 1 can (14 ounces) black beans, drained and rinsed
- 1 cup corn kernels (fresh or frozen)
- 1 cup diced tomatoes
- 1 cup shredded cheddar cheese
- 1/2 cup diced green bell pepper
- Salt and black pepper to taste

For the Pie Crust:

- 1 package (2 crusts) store-bought or homemade pie crust

For Topping:

- Sour cream
- Salsa
- Avocado slices
- Fresh cilantro, chopped

Instructions:

Preheat your oven to 425°F (220°C).
In a large skillet, cook the ground beef or turkey over medium heat until browned. Drain any excess fat.
Add the chopped onion and minced garlic to the skillet. Cook for about 3-5 minutes until the onion is softened.
Stir in the taco seasoning, black beans, corn kernels, diced tomatoes, shredded cheddar cheese, and diced green bell pepper. Cook for an additional 5-7 minutes

until the mixture is heated through and well combined. Season with salt and black pepper to taste. Remove the skillet from heat.
Roll out one pie crust and place it into the bottom of a 9-inch pie dish.
Spoon the Tex-Mex taco filling over the crust.
Roll out the second pie crust and place it over the filling. Seal the edges by crimping them with a fork or your fingers. Cut a few slits in the top crust to allow steam to escape.
Optional: Brush the top crust with a beaten egg for a golden finish.
Place the pie dish on a baking sheet to catch any potential drips and bake in the preheated oven for 30-35 minutes or until the crust is golden brown.
Allow the Tex-Mex taco pot pie to cool for a few minutes before serving. Slice and serve with toppings like sour cream, salsa, avocado slices, and chopped fresh cilantro.

Enjoy the bold and savory flavors of this Tex-Mex-inspired pot pie! Feel free to customize the recipe to your liking, and happy cooking!

Philly Cheesesteak Pot Pie

Ingredients:

For the Filling:

- 1 1/2 pounds thinly sliced beef sirloin or ribeye
- 1 onion, thinly sliced
- 1 green bell pepper, thinly sliced
- 8 ounces mushrooms, sliced
- 2 tablespoons vegetable oil
- 2 tablespoons unsalted butter
- 2 tablespoons all-purpose flour
- 2 cups beef broth
- 1 cup provolone cheese, shredded
- Salt and black pepper to taste

For the Pie Crust:

- 1 package (2 crusts) store-bought or homemade pie crust

Instructions:

Preheat your oven to 425°F (220°C).

In a large skillet, heat the vegetable oil over medium-high heat. Add the thinly sliced beef and cook until browned. Remove the beef from the skillet and set aside.

In the same skillet, add the butter and sauté the sliced onion, green bell pepper, and mushrooms until softened.

Sprinkle the flour over the vegetables and stir to create a roux. Cook for an additional 2-3 minutes.

Gradually whisk in the beef broth, stirring constantly to avoid lumps. Cook until the mixture thickens and becomes smooth.

Return the cooked beef to the skillet and stir until well coated with the broth mixture. Season with salt and black pepper to taste.

Roll out one pie crust and place it into the bottom of a 9-inch pie dish.

Spoon the Philly cheesesteak filling over the crust.

Sprinkle the shredded provolone cheese over the filling.

Roll out the second pie crust and place it over the filling. Seal the edges by crimping them with a fork or your fingers. Cut a few slits in the top crust to allow steam to escape.
Optional: Brush the top crust with a beaten egg for a golden finish.
Place the pie dish on a baking sheet to catch any potential drips and bake in the preheated oven for 30-35 minutes or until the crust is golden brown and the filling is bubbly.
Allow the Philly cheesesteak pot pie to cool for a few minutes before serving.
Slice and enjoy the delicious combination of flavors reminiscent of a classic Philly cheesesteak!

Feel free to customize the recipe to your liking, and happy cooking!

Mediterranean Chickpea Pot Pie

Ingredients:

For the Filling:

- 2 cans (15 ounces each) chickpeas, drained and rinsed
- 1 cup cherry tomatoes, halved
- 1 cup Kalamata olives, pitted and sliced
- 1 cup artichoke hearts, quartered
- 1/2 cup red onion, finely chopped
- 1/2 cup feta cheese, crumbled
- 1/4 cup fresh parsley, chopped
- 2 tablespoons extra virgin olive oil
- 2 cloves garlic, minced
- 1 teaspoon dried oregano
- 1 teaspoon dried thyme
- Salt and black pepper to taste
- Zest and juice of 1 lemon

For the Pie Crust:

- 1 package (2 crusts) store-bought or homemade pie crust

Instructions:

Preheat your oven to 425°F (220°C).
In a large bowl, combine the chickpeas, halved cherry tomatoes, sliced Kalamata olives, quartered artichoke hearts, chopped red onion, crumbled feta cheese, and chopped fresh parsley.
In a small bowl, whisk together the extra virgin olive oil, minced garlic, dried oregano, dried thyme, salt, black pepper, and the zest and juice of one lemon.
Pour the dressing over the chickpea mixture and toss until well coated.
Roll out one pie crust and place it into the bottom of a 9-inch pie dish.
Spoon the Mediterranean chickpea filling over the crust.
Roll out the second pie crust and place it over the filling. Seal the edges by crimping them with a fork or your fingers. Cut a few slits in the top crust to allow steam to escape.
Optional: Brush the top crust with a little extra virgin olive oil for a golden finish.

Place the pie dish on a baking sheet to catch any potential drips and bake in the preheated oven for 25-30 minutes or until the crust is golden brown.
Allow the Mediterranean chickpea pot pie to cool for a few minutes before serving. Enjoy the fresh and vibrant flavors of this Mediterranean-inspired dish!

Feel free to customize the recipe to your liking, and happy cooking!

Pesto Chicken Pot Pie

Ingredients:

For the Filling:

- 2 cups cooked chicken, shredded
- 1 cup carrots, diced
- 1 cup frozen peas
- 1/2 cup red bell pepper, diced
- 1/4 cup unsalted butter
- 1/4 cup all-purpose flour
- 2 cups chicken broth
- 1 cup whole milk
- 1/2 cup pesto sauce
- Salt and black pepper to taste

For the Pie Crust:

- 1 package (2 crusts) store-bought or homemade pie crust

Instructions:

Preheat your oven to 425°F (220°C).
In a large skillet, melt the butter over medium heat. Add the diced carrots, frozen peas, and diced red bell pepper. Cook for about 5-7 minutes until the vegetables are softened.
Stir in the flour to create a roux. Cook for an additional 2-3 minutes to eliminate the raw flour taste.
Gradually whisk in the chicken broth and whole milk, stirring constantly to avoid lumps. Cook the mixture until it thickens and becomes smooth, usually around 5-7 minutes.
Stir in the shredded chicken and pesto sauce. Season with salt and black pepper to taste. Remove the skillet from heat.
Roll out one pie crust and place it into the bottom of a 9-inch pie dish.
Spoon the pesto chicken filling over the crust.

Roll out the second pie crust and place it over the filling. Seal the edges by crimping them with a fork or your fingers. Cut a few slits in the top crust to allow steam to escape.
Optional: Brush the top crust with a beaten egg for a golden finish.
Place the pie dish on a baking sheet to catch any potential drips and bake in the preheated oven for 30-35 minutes or until the crust is golden brown.
Allow the pesto chicken pot pie to cool for a few minutes before serving. Enjoy the delightful combination of flavors with the rich and herby pesto sauce!

Feel free to customize the recipe to your liking, and happy cooking!

Hawaiian Pizza Pot Pie

Ingredients:

For the Filling:

- 1 cup ham, diced
- 1 cup pineapple chunks
- 1/2 cup red bell pepper, diced
- 1/2 cup red onion, diced
- 1 cup shredded mozzarella cheese
- 1/2 cup pizza sauce
- 1 tablespoon olive oil
- 1 teaspoon dried oregano
- 1/2 teaspoon garlic powder
- Salt and black pepper to taste

For the Pie Crust:

- 1 package (2 crusts) store-bought or homemade pie crust

Instructions:

Preheat your oven to 425°F (220°C).
In a skillet, heat olive oil over medium heat. Add the diced red onion and red bell pepper. Sauté for 3-5 minutes until softened.
Add the diced ham to the skillet and cook for an additional 3-5 minutes until the ham is lightly browned.
Stir in the pineapple chunks, pizza sauce, dried oregano, garlic powder, salt, and black pepper. Cook for another 2-3 minutes until all ingredients are well combined. Remove the skillet from heat.
Roll out one pie crust and place it into the bottom of a 9-inch pie dish.
Spoon the Hawaiian pizza filling over the crust.
Sprinkle the shredded mozzarella cheese over the filling.
Roll out the second pie crust and place it over the filling. Seal the edges by crimping them with a fork or your fingers. Cut a few slits in the top crust to allow steam to escape.

Optional: Brush the top crust with a little olive oil for a golden finish.

Place the pie dish on a baking sheet to catch any potential drips and bake in the preheated oven for 25-30 minutes or until the crust is golden brown.

Allow the Hawaiian pizza pot pie to cool for a few minutes before serving. Enjoy the tropical flavors of this pizza-inspired pot pie!

Feel free to customize the recipe with your favorite pizza toppings or sauce. Happy cooking!

Chicken Pesto Pot Pie

Ingredients:

For the Filling:

- 2 cups cooked chicken, shredded
- 1 cup carrots, diced
- 1 cup frozen peas
- 1/2 cup red bell pepper, diced
- 1/4 cup unsalted butter
- 1/4 cup all-purpose flour
- 2 cups chicken broth
- 1 cup whole milk
- 1/2 cup pesto sauce
- Salt and black pepper to taste

For the Pie Crust:

- 1 package (2 crusts) store-bought or homemade pie crust

Instructions:

Preheat your oven to 425°F (220°C).
In a large skillet, melt the butter over medium heat. Add the diced carrots, frozen peas, and diced red bell pepper. Cook for about 5-7 minutes until the vegetables are softened.
Stir in the flour to create a roux. Cook for an additional 2-3 minutes to eliminate the raw flour taste.
Gradually whisk in the chicken broth and whole milk, stirring constantly to avoid lumps. Cook the mixture until it thickens and becomes smooth, usually around 5-7 minutes.
Stir in the shredded chicken and pesto sauce. Season with salt and black pepper to taste. Remove the skillet from heat.
Roll out one pie crust and place it into the bottom of a 9-inch pie dish.
Spoon the pesto chicken filling over the crust.

Roll out the second pie crust and place it over the filling. Seal the edges by crimping them with a fork or your fingers. Cut a few slits in the top crust to allow steam to escape.

Optional: Brush the top crust with a beaten egg for a golden finish.

Place the pie dish on a baking sheet to catch any potential drips and bake in the preheated oven for 30-35 minutes or until the crust is golden brown.

Allow the pesto chicken pot pie to cool for a few minutes before serving. Enjoy the delightful combination of flavors with the rich and herby pesto sauce!

Feel free to customize the recipe to your liking, and happy cooking!

Sloppy Joe Pot Pie

Ingredients:

For the Filling:

- 1 pound ground beef
- 1 onion, finely chopped
- 1 green bell pepper, diced
- 2 cloves garlic, minced
- 1 cup tomato sauce
- 1/4 cup ketchup
- 2 tablespoons brown sugar
- 1 tablespoon Worcestershire sauce
- 1 teaspoon Dijon mustard
- Salt and black pepper to taste

For the Pie Crust:

- 1 package (2 crusts) store-bought or homemade pie crust

Instructions:

Preheat your oven to 425°F (220°C).
In a large skillet, cook the ground beef over medium heat until browned. Drain any excess fat.
Add the chopped onion, diced green bell pepper, and minced garlic to the skillet. Cook for about 3-5 minutes until the vegetables are softened.
Stir in the tomato sauce, ketchup, brown sugar, Worcestershire sauce, Dijon mustard, salt, and black pepper. Simmer the mixture for 10-12 minutes until it thickens and the flavors meld.
Roll out one pie crust and place it into the bottom of a 9-inch pie dish.
Spoon the Sloppy Joe filling over the crust.
Roll out the second pie crust and place it over the filling. Seal the edges by crimping them with a fork or your fingers. Cut a few slits in the top crust to allow steam to escape.
Optional: Brush the top crust with a beaten egg for a golden finish.

Place the pie dish on a baking sheet to catch any potential drips and bake in the preheated oven for 30-35 minutes or until the crust is golden brown.
Allow the Sloppy Joe pot pie to cool for a few minutes before serving. Slice and enjoy the hearty and savory flavors of this comfort food twist!

Feel free to customize the recipe by adding cheese or your favorite Sloppy Joe toppings.

Happy cooking!

Mushroom and Leek Pot Pie

Ingredients:

For the Filling:

- 2 cups cremini mushrooms, sliced
- 2 cups button mushrooms, sliced
- 2 leeks, cleaned and thinly sliced
- 3 tablespoons unsalted butter
- 1/4 cup all-purpose flour
- 2 cups vegetable broth
- 1 cup whole milk or heavy cream
- 1/2 cup white wine (optional)
- 2 cloves garlic, minced
- 1 teaspoon dried thyme
- Salt and black pepper to taste
- 1/4 cup fresh parsley, chopped

For the Pie Crust:

- 1 package (2 crusts) store-bought or homemade pie crust

Instructions:

Preheat your oven to 425°F (220°C).
In a large skillet, melt the butter over medium heat. Add the sliced mushrooms and leeks. Cook for about 8-10 minutes until the vegetables are softened and the mushrooms release their moisture.
Stir in the minced garlic and cook for an additional 1-2 minutes until fragrant.
Sprinkle the flour over the mushroom and leek mixture, stirring to create a roux. Cook for 2-3 minutes to eliminate the raw flour taste.
Gradually whisk in the vegetable broth, milk or cream, and white wine (if using), stirring constantly to avoid lumps. Cook the mixture until it thickens and becomes smooth, usually around 5-7 minutes.
Add the dried thyme, salt, black pepper, and chopped fresh parsley to the skillet. Stir until the ingredients are well combined. Remove the skillet from heat.
Roll out one pie crust and place it into the bottom of a 9-inch pie dish.
Spoon the mushroom and leek filling over the crust.

Roll out the second pie crust and place it over the filling. Seal the edges by crimping them with a fork or your fingers. Cut a few slits in the top crust to allow steam to escape.

Optional: Brush the top crust with a beaten egg for a golden finish.

Place the pie dish on a baking sheet to catch any potential drips and bake in the preheated oven for 30-35 minutes or until the crust is golden brown.

Allow the mushroom and leek pot pie to cool for a few minutes before serving. Enjoy the earthy and savory flavors of this delicious pot pie!

Feel free to customize the recipe to your liking, and happy cooking!

Spinach and Artichoke Pot Pie

Ingredients:

For the Filling:

- 2 cups fresh spinach, chopped
- 1 can (14 ounces) artichoke hearts, drained and chopped
- 1 cup cream cheese, softened
- 1 cup shredded mozzarella cheese
- 1/2 cup grated Parmesan cheese
- 1/4 cup mayonnaise
- 2 cloves garlic, minced
- 1 teaspoon dried oregano
- Salt and black pepper to taste

For the Pie Crust:

- 1 package (2 crusts) store-bought or homemade pie crust

Instructions:

Preheat your oven to 425°F (220°C).
In a mixing bowl, combine the chopped fresh spinach, chopped artichoke hearts, softened cream cheese, shredded mozzarella cheese, grated Parmesan cheese, mayonnaise, minced garlic, dried oregano, salt, and black pepper. Mix well until all ingredients are evenly combined.
Roll out one pie crust and place it into the bottom of a 9-inch pie dish.
Spoon the spinach and artichoke filling over the crust.
Roll out the second pie crust and place it over the filling. Seal the edges by crimping them with a fork or your fingers. Cut a few slits in the top crust to allow steam to escape.
Optional: Brush the top crust with a beaten egg for a golden finish.
Place the pie dish on a baking sheet to catch any potential drips and bake in the preheated oven for 25-30 minutes or until the crust is golden brown.
Allow the spinach and artichoke pot pie to cool for a few minutes before serving.
Enjoy the creamy and flavorful combination of spinach and artichoke in a comforting pot pie!

Feel free to customize the recipe to your liking, and happy cooking!

Italian Sausage and Peppers Pot Pie

Ingredients:

For the Filling:

- 1 pound Italian sausage, casings removed and crumbled
- 1 onion, thinly sliced
- 2 bell peppers (any color), thinly sliced
- 2 cloves garlic, minced
- 1 can (14 ounces) diced tomatoes, drained
- 1/4 cup tomato paste
- 1 teaspoon dried oregano
- 1 teaspoon dried basil
- Salt and black pepper to taste
- 1 cup shredded mozzarella cheese

For the Pie Crust:

- 1 package (2 crusts) store-bought or homemade pie crust

Instructions:

Preheat your oven to 425°F (220°C).
In a large skillet, cook the crumbled Italian sausage over medium-high heat until browned. Remove any excess fat.
Add the thinly sliced onion, bell peppers, and minced garlic to the skillet. Cook for about 5-7 minutes until the vegetables are softened.
Stir in the drained diced tomatoes, tomato paste, dried oregano, dried basil, salt, and black pepper. Cook for an additional 5 minutes to allow the flavors to meld. Remove the skillet from heat.
Roll out one pie crust and place it into the bottom of a 9-inch pie dish.
Spoon the Italian sausage and peppers filling over the crust.
Sprinkle the shredded mozzarella cheese over the filling.
Roll out the second pie crust and place it over the filling. Seal the edges by crimping them with a fork or your fingers. Cut a few slits in the top crust to allow steam to escape.

Optional: Brush the top crust with a beaten egg for a golden finish.
Place the pie dish on a baking sheet to catch any potential drips and bake in the preheated oven for 30-35 minutes or until the crust is golden brown.
Allow the Italian Sausage and Peppers pot pie to cool for a few minutes before serving. Enjoy the robust and savory flavors of this hearty pot pie!

Feel free to customize the recipe to your liking, and happy cooking!

Bacon and Egg Breakfast Pot Pie

Ingredients:

For the Filling:

- 8 slices bacon, cooked and crumbled
- 1 cup shredded cheddar cheese
- 6 large eggs
- 1/4 cup milk
- Salt and black pepper to taste
- Chopped chives or green onions for garnish (optional)

For the Pie Crust:

- 1 package (2 crusts) store-bought or homemade pie crust

Instructions:

Preheat your oven to 375°F (190°C).
Roll out one pie crust and place it into the bottom of a 9-inch pie dish.
In a bowl, whisk together the eggs, milk, salt, and black pepper until well combined.
Sprinkle half of the crumbled bacon and half of the shredded cheddar cheese over the pie crust.
Pour the egg mixture over the bacon and cheese.
Sprinkle the remaining bacon and cheese over the egg mixture.
Roll out the second pie crust and place it over the filling. Seal the edges by crimping them with a fork or your fingers. Cut a few slits in the top crust to allow steam to escape.
Optional: Brush the top crust with a beaten egg for a golden finish.
Place the pie dish on a baking sheet to catch any potential drips and bake in the preheated oven for 25-30 minutes or until the crust is golden brown and the eggs are set.
Allow the Bacon and Egg Breakfast pot pie to cool for a few minutes before serving.
Garnish with chopped chives or green onions if desired. Slice and enjoy a delicious breakfast pot pie with the classic combination of bacon and eggs!

Feel free to customize the recipe by adding your favorite breakfast ingredients. Happy cooking!

Chicken and Waffle Pot Pie

Ingredients:

For the Filling:

- 2 cups cooked chicken, shredded
- 1 cup frozen peas
- 1 cup carrots, diced
- 1/2 cup celery, diced
- 1/4 cup unsalted butter
- 1/4 cup all-purpose flour
- 2 cups chicken broth
- 1 cup whole milk
- 1 teaspoon dried thyme
- Salt and black pepper to taste

For the Waffle Topping:

- 2 cups waffle mix (prepared according to package instructions)
- 1/2 cup shredded cheddar cheese
- 1/4 cup chopped green onions (optional)

Instructions:

Preheat your oven to 425°F (220°C).
In a large skillet, melt the butter over medium heat. Add the diced carrots, diced celery, and frozen peas. Cook for about 5-7 minutes until the vegetables are softened.
Stir in the flour to create a roux. Cook for an additional 2-3 minutes to eliminate the raw flour taste.
Gradually whisk in the chicken broth and whole milk, stirring constantly to avoid lumps. Cook the mixture until it thickens and becomes smooth, usually around 5-7 minutes.
Add the shredded chicken, dried thyme, salt, and black pepper to the skillet. Stir until all ingredients are well combined. Remove the skillet from heat.

In a separate bowl, prepare the waffle mix according to the package instructions.
Stir in the shredded cheddar cheese and chopped green onions if using.
Roll out one pie crust and place it into the bottom of a 9-inch pie dish.
Spoon the chicken and vegetable filling over the crust.
Pour the prepared waffle mix over the filling, spreading it evenly.
Optional: Garnish the waffle topping with additional shredded cheese or chopped green onions.
Place the pie dish on a baking sheet to catch any potential drips and bake in the preheated oven for 25-30 minutes or until the waffle topping is golden brown.
Allow the Chicken and Waffle pot pie to cool for a few minutes before serving.
Enjoy this unique and comforting twist on a classic dish!

Feel free to customize the recipe to your liking, and happy cooking!

Buffalo Cauliflower Mac and Cheese Pot Pie

Ingredients:

For the Filling:

- 1 head cauliflower, cut into florets
- 2 tablespoons olive oil
- Salt and black pepper to taste
- 1/2 cup buffalo sauce
- 2 cups cooked macaroni or pasta of choice
- 2 cups shredded sharp cheddar cheese
- 1 cup milk
- 1/4 cup unsalted butter
- 1/4 cup all-purpose flour
- 1/2 teaspoon garlic powder
- 1/2 teaspoon onion powder

For the Pie Crust:

- 1 package (2 crusts) store-bought or homemade pie crust

Instructions:

Preheat your oven to 425°F (220°C).
Toss the cauliflower florets with olive oil, salt, and black pepper. Spread them out on a baking sheet and roast in the preheated oven for 20-25 minutes or until golden brown and tender.
In a large saucepan, melt the butter over medium heat. Stir in the flour to create a roux. Cook for 2-3 minutes to eliminate the raw flour taste.
Gradually whisk in the milk, stirring constantly to avoid lumps. Cook the mixture until it thickens and becomes smooth, usually around 5-7 minutes.
Stir in the shredded cheddar cheese, garlic powder, and onion powder. Continue stirring until the cheese is melted and the sauce is smooth.
Add the buffalo sauce to the cheese sauce, mixing well.
In a large mixing bowl, combine the roasted cauliflower, cooked macaroni, and the buffalo cheese sauce. Mix until all ingredients are evenly coated.
Roll out one pie crust and place it into the bottom of a 9-inch pie dish.
Spoon the Buffalo Cauliflower Mac and Cheese filling over the crust.

Roll out the second pie crust and place it over the filling. Seal the edges by crimping them with a fork or your fingers. Cut a few slits in the top crust to allow steam to escape.

Optional: Brush the top crust with a beaten egg for a golden finish.

Place the pie dish on a baking sheet to catch any potential drips and bake in the preheated oven for 30-35 minutes or until the crust is golden brown.

Allow the Buffalo Cauliflower Mac and Cheese pot pie to cool for a few minutes before serving. Enjoy the spicy and cheesy goodness of this creative and flavorful dish!

Feel free to customize the recipe to your liking, and happy cooking!

Teriyaki Salmon Pot Pie

Ingredients:

For the Filling:

- 2 cups cooked salmon, flaked
- 1 cup broccoli florets, blanched
- 1 cup carrots, diced and blanched
- 1/2 cup red bell pepper, diced
- 1/4 cup teriyaki sauce
- 1 tablespoon soy sauce
- 2 tablespoons sesame oil
- 2 cloves garlic, minced
- 1 tablespoon ginger, grated
- 1 tablespoon cornstarch (optional, for thickening)
- Salt and black pepper to taste

For the Pie Crust:

- 1 package (2 crusts) store-bought or homemade pie crust

Instructions:

Preheat your oven to 425°F (220°C).
In a large bowl, combine the flaked cooked salmon, blanched broccoli florets, blanched diced carrots, and diced red bell pepper.
In a small bowl, whisk together the teriyaki sauce, soy sauce, sesame oil, minced garlic, grated ginger, and cornstarch (if using).
Pour the teriyaki sauce mixture over the salmon and vegetable mixture. Toss until well coated. Season with salt and black pepper to taste.
Roll out one pie crust and place it into the bottom of a 9-inch pie dish.
Spoon the Teriyaki Salmon filling over the crust.
Roll out the second pie crust and place it over the filling. Seal the edges by crimping them with a fork or your fingers. Cut a few slits in the top crust to allow steam to escape.

Optional: Brush the top crust with a little sesame oil for added flavor and a golden finish.

Place the pie dish on a baking sheet to catch any potential drips and bake in the preheated oven for 25-30 minutes or until the crust is golden brown.

Allow the Teriyaki Salmon pot pie to cool for a few minutes before serving. Enjoy the delightful fusion of teriyaki flavors with the richness of salmon in this unique pot pie!

Feel free to customize the recipe to your liking, and happy cooking!

Southwest Chicken Pot Pie

Ingredients:

For the Filling:

- 2 cups cooked chicken, shredded
- 1 cup black beans, drained and rinsed
- 1 cup corn kernels (fresh or frozen)
- 1 cup diced tomatoes
- 1/2 cup diced red bell pepper
- 1/2 cup diced green bell pepper
- 1/2 cup diced red onion
- 1 cup shredded cheddar cheese
- 1/4 cup chopped fresh cilantro
- 1 teaspoon ground cumin
- 1 teaspoon chili powder
- 1/2 teaspoon garlic powder
- Salt and black pepper to taste

For the Pie Crust:

- 1 package (2 crusts) store-bought or homemade pie crust

Instructions:

Preheat your oven to 425°F (220°C).
In a large bowl, combine the shredded cooked chicken, black beans, corn kernels, diced tomatoes, diced red and green bell peppers, diced red onion, shredded cheddar cheese, chopped fresh cilantro, ground cumin, chili powder, garlic powder, salt, and black pepper. Mix well until all ingredients are evenly distributed.
Roll out one pie crust and place it into the bottom of a 9-inch pie dish.
Spoon the Southwest Chicken filling over the crust.
Roll out the second pie crust and place it over the filling. Seal the edges by crimping them with a fork or your fingers. Cut a few slits in the top crust to allow steam to escape.

Optional: Brush the top crust with a beaten egg for a golden finish.
Place the pie dish on a baking sheet to catch any potential drips and bake in the preheated oven for 30-35 minutes or until the crust is golden brown.
Allow the Southwest Chicken pot pie to cool for a few minutes before serving.
Enjoy the bold and spicy flavors of this southwestern-inspired pot pie!

Feel free to customize the recipe to your liking, and happy cooking!

Quiche Lorraine Pot Pie

Ingredients:

For the Filling:

- 1 cup bacon, cooked and crumbled
- 1 cup Gruyère or Swiss cheese, shredded
- 1/2 cup caramelized onions
- 4 large eggs
- 1 cup heavy cream
- 1/2 teaspoon salt
- 1/4 teaspoon black pepper
- 1/4 teaspoon nutmeg (optional)

For the Pie Crust:

- 1 package (2 crusts) store-bought or homemade pie crust

Instructions:

Preheat your oven to 375°F (190°C).
Roll out one pie crust and place it into the bottom of a 9-inch pie dish.
In a bowl, whisk together the eggs, heavy cream, salt, black pepper, and nutmeg (if using) until well combined.
Sprinkle half of the bacon, half of the shredded Gruyère or Swiss cheese, and half of the caramelized onions over the pie crust.
Pour half of the egg mixture over the bacon, cheese, and onions.
Repeat the layers with the remaining bacon, cheese, and caramelized onions.
Pour the remaining egg mixture over the top.
Roll out the second pie crust and place it over the filling. Seal the edges by crimping them with a fork or your fingers. Cut a few slits in the top crust to allow steam to escape.
Optional: Brush the top crust with a beaten egg for a golden finish.
Place the pie dish on a baking sheet to catch any potential drips and bake in the preheated oven for 35-40 minutes or until the crust is golden brown and the filling is set.

Allow the Quiche Lorraine pot pie to cool for a few minutes before serving. Slice and enjoy the classic flavors of Quiche Lorraine in pot pie form!

Feel free to customize the recipe by adding other ingredients like spinach, mushrooms, or herbs to suit your taste. Happy cooking!

Cheesy Broccoli and Rice Pot Pie

Ingredients:

For the Filling:

- 2 cups broccoli florets, blanched
- 1 cup cooked white rice
- 1 cup shredded cheddar cheese
- 1/2 cup diced onions
- 1/4 cup unsalted butter
- 1/4 cup all-purpose flour
- 2 cups milk
- 1 cup vegetable or chicken broth
- 1 teaspoon Dijon mustard
- Salt and black pepper to taste

For the Pie Crust:

- 1 package (2 crusts) store-bought or homemade pie crust

Instructions:

Preheat your oven to 425°F (220°C).
In a large skillet, melt the butter over medium heat. Add the diced onions and cook until softened.
Stir in the flour to create a roux. Cook for 2-3 minutes to eliminate the raw flour taste.
Gradually whisk in the milk and vegetable or chicken broth, stirring constantly to avoid lumps. Cook the mixture until it thickens and becomes smooth, usually around 5-7 minutes.
Stir in the Dijon mustard, shredded cheddar cheese, salt, and black pepper. Continue stirring until the cheese is melted and the sauce is smooth.
In a large bowl, combine the blanched broccoli florets, cooked white rice, and the cheese sauce. Mix well until all ingredients are evenly coated.
Roll out one pie crust and place it into the bottom of a 9-inch pie dish.
Spoon the Cheesy Broccoli and Rice filling over the crust.

Roll out the second pie crust and place it over the filling. Seal the edges by crimping them with a fork or your fingers. Cut a few slits in the top crust to allow steam to escape.

Optional: Brush the top crust with a beaten egg for a golden finish.

Place the pie dish on a baking sheet to catch any potential drips and bake in the preheated oven for 30-35 minutes or until the crust is golden brown.

Allow the Cheesy Broccoli and Rice pot pie to cool for a few minutes before serving. Enjoy the comforting combination of cheesy goodness with broccoli and rice!

Feel free to customize the recipe by adding other vegetables or spices to suit your taste.

Happy cooking!

Caramelized Onion and Gruyere Pot Pie

Ingredients:

For the Filling:

- 4 large onions, thinly sliced
- 2 tablespoons unsalted butter
- 1 tablespoon olive oil
- 1 teaspoon sugar
- 1/4 cup dry white wine (optional)
- 2 cups Gruyère cheese, shredded
- 1/4 cup all-purpose flour
- 2 cups vegetable or beef broth
- Salt and black pepper to taste
- 1 teaspoon fresh thyme leaves (optional)

For the Pie Crust:

- 1 package (2 crusts) store-bought or homemade pie crust

Instructions:

Preheat your oven to 425°F (220°C).
In a large skillet, heat the butter and olive oil over medium heat. Add the thinly sliced onions and sugar. Cook, stirring occasionally, until the onions are caramelized and golden brown. This process may take about 20-30 minutes.
If using, pour in the dry white wine to deglaze the skillet, scraping up any browned bits from the bottom. Allow the wine to cook off, leaving the onions with a rich flavor.
Stir in the flour and cook for an additional 2-3 minutes to eliminate the raw flour taste.
Gradually whisk in the vegetable or beef broth, stirring constantly to avoid lumps. Cook the mixture until it thickens and becomes smooth, usually around 5-7 minutes.
Remove the skillet from heat and stir in the shredded Gruyère cheese until melted. Season with salt and black pepper to taste. If desired, add fresh thyme leaves for extra flavor.
Roll out one pie crust and place it into the bottom of a 9-inch pie dish.

Spoon the Caramelized Onion and Gruyère filling over the crust.

Roll out the second pie crust and place it over the filling. Seal the edges by crimping them with a fork or your fingers. Cut a few slits in the top crust to allow steam to escape.

Optional: Brush the top crust with a beaten egg for a golden finish.

Place the pie dish on a baking sheet to catch any potential drips and bake in the preheated oven for 30-35 minutes or until the crust is golden brown.

Allow the Caramelized Onion and Gruyère pot pie to cool for a few minutes before serving. Enjoy the rich and savory flavors of this delightful dish!

Feel free to customize the recipe to your liking, and happy cooking!

www.ingramcontent.com/pod-product-compliance
Lightning Source LLC
LaVergne TN
LVHW081614060526
838201LV00054B/2245